LOSING
to
WIN

Shondra N. Davis

ISBN 979-8-89243-919-0 (paperback)
ISBN 979-8-89243-920-6 (digital)

Christian Faith Publishing
832 Park Avenue
Meadville, PA 16335
www.christianfaithpublishing.com

Printed in the United States of America

PREFACE

This was developed using actual journal entries inspired by God while recovering from the greatest loss of my life, a marriage irretrievably broken. My prayer is that this literature will find its way into your hands and heart and encourage you who have suffered loss, disappointment, or a setback to live again! Trust God with your life, and He will make LIFE happen! It is not enough to merely exist but is important that we LIVE the best life God has to offer you! Sometimes you must lose to gain! Be determined to WIN! Be *W*illing *I*nside to *N*ever give up!

It was the day before Thanksgiving 2017 and just enough time to do one last pre-thanksgiving dinner run! "Pick up the cake, make bank deposit, pick up meds, and final stop to the grocery store!" Those were the thoughts that repeated in my head as I hurried out the door. "Thank God for the handicap sticker," I exclaimed as we pulled into Kroger parking lot on Mall Boulevard. The store was crowded, and it wasn't even noon yet! I'd been suffering with pain to my left knee as a result of the car wreck I'd been injured in in January and walking long distances would only make it worse.

Heading to the drink aisle, I caught a glimpse of a previous employee(now friend). I proceeded to the frozen foods section where she was and greeted her with a hug and kiss! We were so excited to see each other because we both had walked similar paths on this year. As we talked, I couldn't believe my ears but truly believed all she was saying. I knew this was God! It was as if God divinely placed Tanya right there for such a time as this!

And that's when it happened! That's when the Holy Spirit spoke clearly saying, "LOSING TO GAIN!"

I am Shondra Nicole Stewart, soon to return to Shondra Nicole Davis in the next eight days. "What do you mean?" I'm sure is the thought in your mind right now. And even as I type, God is giving me an even greater insight and understanding of what is going on.

This year has been a year of significant loss. In January, I was injured in a car wreck while heading to a meeting. I'll never forget that day. I was the Director of Operations for one of the leading home health agencies in the United States. I refrain from sharing the name for confidentiality purposes. Anyway, I was doing great! I was living the American dream: significant and successful business-woman, married to the first guy I dated in college, daughter set to be the valedictorian of her graduating class, had just built and purchased our first home, a strong and faithful relationship with the Lord! Life couldn't get any better than this! But that one day, that one instance on January 27, 2017 changed everything! I was literally laid flat on my back after being rear-ended by a SUV while sitting at a traffic light. Upon impact, I immediately knew I was about to suffer loss in order to gain, but I was by no means aware of the details that would unfold and occur on this journey!

"Give not that which is holy unto the dogs, neither cast ye your pearls before swine, lest they trample them under their feet, and turn again and rend you" (Matthew 7:6).

I realized on this morning as I scrolled through social media pictures and posts that there are so many hurting people. I see wives crying out for the love of their husbands. I see people standing without the ones who once proclaimed to have such great love for them. I see others struggling to get their life back, crying out to get their joy back, and I can't help but wonder, "What happened? Where did we go wrong? Father, what is going on?"

And as I see all of these things, I can't help but to also see me. Then the thought gently crept into my mind: People somehow have a tendency to misunderstand the purpose of people entering our lives. What do I mean?

Oftentimes we mistake those who came into our lives for a reason as meaning to be there for a season, those who came for a season as meant for a lifetime. Then we are trying so hard to hold on to the reasons and seasons that we miss the lifetimes! Wow!

So I pray for serenity—not in the way that we once knew it but on a greater level. For it is in serenity that true healing and greater living can and will begin! You deserve LIFE! You deserve PEACE! You deserve JOY!

Prayer

God, grant us the serenity to discern and accept the true purpose of relationships, encounters, and experiences in our lives.

Lord, help us to NOT give our pearls to the swine but to hold fast to only those things that will enhance our lives to what is that good and perfect will that you have for us.

For it is only in your will that we will find and experience our greatest heart's desires! Amen.

LOSING

Last night, we had an argument; yes, another argument. These seem to be occurring more frequently now. I stepped out of character and put my hands around his neck. It boils down to the same age-old issues of our marriage: disrespect, lack of regard, negligence—evidence that neither of us are truly happy. He admitted I'm a good wife but can't receive that I need for him to be a better husband to me. LOVE ME! CARE FOR ME! NURTURE AND HONOR ME! CONSIDER ME! PROVIDE THE EMOTIONAL THINGS I NEED FROM YOU AS MY HUSBAND! NO MONEY! NO FORM OR FASHION! JUST YOUR HEART!

Anyway, I had two dreams last night. In each dream, someone was trying to hurt me, but it did not work. One was of a man raising his hand to hit me, but his arm literally broke into two pieces. I had to take him to the emergency room for care. The other was of a guy trying to hurt me in four different ways, but it did not work. What are you trying to tell me God? How can the thing I prayed for, waited for, believed and trusted you for be deteriorating right before my eyes? How is it that we are losing while so many around us are rapidly experiencing growth?

SCRIPTURE

> "I returned and saw under the sun that the race is not given to the swift, nor the battle to the strong, nor bread to the wise, nor riches to men of understanding, nor favor to men of skill; but time and chance happen to them all" (Ecclesiastes 9:11, KJV.)

WINNING

"Have you ever needed someone so bad? But he ain't willing to make it last. Sometimes you got to lose to win again!"

As I awakened on this morning, these words sang in my head. I googled because I couldn't remember the entire song, and what were they? Lyrics to Fantasia Barrino's song, "Lose to Win." And that was me. I made my ex-husband's life my life. I gave my all. I stopped celebrating my life and my accomplishments or altered celebrations to "build up his manhood." What do I mean? I can remember getting my second pay raise at work after we were married and having to search for the right words to use and the right timing to tell him about it. Why? Because I knew good for me would be counted as a negative for him. My successes were never met with immediate praise. It would not be until days later that he would be able to get over himself and give me the appropriate congratulations I was due. I always knew positive for me somehow magnified the negatives he was experiencing in life. He somehow always found fault in what brought me joy whether it be gifts or whatever.

So I lost my true ability to celebrate myself.

I sometimes now have to search and wonder what do I REALLY like, what are my TRUE heart's desires?

So how did I win?

All through the night, I had visions of my now, visions of my future! I now have the man of my dreams not just in words but also in deeds. I now have the ability and desire to celebrate myself and all my accomplishments. Attached is the poem I sent to my true love on this morning. I am so determined to focus on my lifetime in front of me. I celebrate LIFE freely. For instance, this Thanksgiving break was my daughter's first stay at home since she left for college, and I wanted to celebrate it! I wanted to make her feel extra special when she arrived home. So what did I do? I decorated, WE decorated her room with streamers and balloons. We hung a big golden balloon bouquet that read "YAY" at the head of her bed, hung streamers from her closet to her mirror, and taped more balloons saying "WELCOME BACK" to her foot posts of her bed. We celebrated her first arrival home from college! And not once was I told I was doing too much. Instead my new life partner stalked the aisles of Wal-Mart to make sure we had everything needed to make Erin feel special.

I have gained the ability to once again celebrate life! It is the little things that make life worth living!

> **Gift:** "This above all: To thine own self be true." Do not be afraid to be who and how God created you to be! God has graced each of us with gifts and most importantly, the gift of life! Life is meant to be enjoyed! Life is meant to be good! Life is meant to be lived in a manner to bring Glory to Our God!

Celebrate YOU!

SCRIPTURE

> "I praise (I celebrate) you because I am fearfully and wonderfully made; your works are wonderful, and that I know quite well" (Psalm 139:14).

CHOOSE WISELY

As I awakened on this morning, I began to seek and search for the purpose and message God would give me for today. The lyrics of "Lose to Win" slowly faded away. Then came, "You've been scared of love and what it did to you." So of course, I became alarmed.

"Wait God! I thought we got beyond this yesterday! What do you mean? Why is this song playing in my head, in my spirit?" I thought I was there. Last night, as we drove back to my hometown from taking my daughter back to college, I opened up to my love and shared with him deep secrets. I shared with him that it was only my faith in God that was getting me through and assuring me that I won't be this way always. I praised him and thanked him for being the strong man he is—the man who has stood beside me throughout this entire ordeal. I acknowledged the spirit of patience in him that I know could only come from God. I thanked him because I know any other man would have turned in the opposite direction by now. So... why? Why am I hearing this song about fear? I denounced fear, at least I thought. What I came to realize is that it is a choice, day by day, and sometimes moment by moment. So TODAY, I choose NOT to fear!

On today, I choose to stand in the liberty that Christ has granted me. I anticipate what is ahead knowing that my best is truly yet to come.

Gift: CHOOSE to be BRAVE! CHOOSE to be BOLD! CHOOSE to be FREE!

SCRIPTURE

"So do not fear, for I am with you; do not be dismayed, for I am your God. I will strengthen you and help you; I will uphold you with my righteous right hand" (Isaiah 41:10, NIV).

CHOICES

As my day comes to a close, I realize today was full of choices. I was lead to find out the truth about a situation that occurred nearly fourteen years ago. I was a little nervous as I approached the receptionist at the Department of Child Support Services but knew it had to be done. I had to find out the truth behind the heartache caused to myself and my child. In 2003, I received a devastating call that a paternity test would be performed for my five-year-old daughter. I truly didn't understand why because nothing had been hidden from my ex-lover (her now acting father.) I remember slumping down on the bathroom floor in disarray and utter unbelief, and that's when the voice spoke to me saying, "I am using them to answer your prayers." Understanding Immediately, I submitted to what was being requested. Let's just say lives were changed and relationships were broken following the receipt of the DNA results. Within the past few months, I was told the reason the paternity test was requested. It's sad when someone can make you question your own credibility even when you know you are innocent. The receptionist explained the case had been no fault of my own but had been opened by the State Department of Community Health. Walking away with my questions answered, I realized I had to make a choice. I could either become enraged because of the information I was given, or I could choose to move forward in forgiveness. I could choose to reopen wounds of the past, or I could keep what I'd already gained and continue to heal. I chose to forgive. I passed the information along and made it clear that I refuse to relive any past hurts or pains. And this is when my day of choices began.

Today was all about choices: choices on how to act and react, choices on how to be.

While in the nail shop, a middle-aged lady gave me an evil eye. In one glance, I could tell she was dissatisfied with the service she was receiving, but I chose to smile. I chose not to join her bandwagon of anger and instead spread joy. It obviously worked. Soon, she was complimenting my nail color and singing the technician praises of thanks. One smile over one frown altered the day positively for four individuals.

Later in the evening, my body felt as if it was turning cartwheels, and a leaky faucet had been turned on. I was suffering from a severe cold accompanied by fever and chills, but a paint night had been scheduled to bid farewell to one of my closest friends. I could have easily cancelled our plans, but instead, I chose to medicate myself and move forward. And I am so happy I did! Not once did I sneeze, cough, etc. My mind was given the opportunity to paint, sip, dance, and most importantly, RELAX. Love songs played reminding me of my ex-husband during our courtship, but I chose to not dwell in the past. I shook the thoughts off and preceded on with our FunDay on a MonDay.

We must realize that life is full of choices, and it is often our choices that shape our reality. So what will you choose today? Will you choose joy? Will you choose peace? Will you choose to be free and to be all who God created you to be?

If you're wondering how I gained from my choices, I gained freedom from an unintentional lie. My daughter gained a relationship with her biological father. And I gained peaceful reminder that there was no reason to doubt myself!

SCRIPTURE

"But choose ye this day who you will serve" (Joshua 24:15).

Will we serve the thoughts of our past? Will we serve hidden agendas, bitter ways? Or will we choose the things of God that will lead to a fulfilling joy and peace?

Choose to Gain!!!! Choose to WIN!!!!

HUMBLE IS THE WAY

"Have you ever been put in a situation to humble you? Well, this is it!"

Those are the words that snatched me out of my sleep. It's 3:45 a.m., two days before my court date, two days before the divorce is legally finalized, two days before my name is restored back to Shondra Nicole Davis. As I exited the bathroom, my eyes caught a glimpse of the stairs, and that's when the thought crept into my head. I still somehow expected for him to walk up those stairs at some point and put up some type of fight for me, for our marriage. But the song gently reminds me that he wasn't willing to make it last. Sometimes you've got to lose to win again. Yes, I lost my dream. Yes, I lost the marriage I thought would last forever. Yes, I lost being married to a man who did not love me how I loved him, but humble is the way.

Humble: (1) not proud or haughty, not arrogant or assertive. (2) reflecting, expressing, or offered in a spirit of deference or submission. (Webster's Online Dictionary)

"Humble yourselves therefore under the mighty hand of God that he may exalt you in due time"—begins to ring in my head, in my Spirit. One may wonder how can God require you to be humble during such a time as this. It even seems unfair sometimes. You are the one who gave it your all! You loved, honored, and respected just as you vowed to do! You were faithful! You forgave! You hung in there for better and for the worst! You gave it your best shot! You covered! Yet, your spouse still left. He/she still told you that your best was not enough—that in itself is enough my friend to send anyone into a raging madness. But God still whispers to you, "Be humble."

It is important that we not seek vengeance of our own account. Let me validate your feelings: The pain, the frustration, every emotion is real! And YOU have every right to feel what you feel! But you also must CHOOSE (there's that word again) the right way. The power of choice is so great now. When the Bible says to humble yourself under God's mighty hand, He is simply telling you to let Him handle the situation. Don't take matters into your own hands. Don't be consumed by emotions and negative thoughts. Instead, know that this is not your battle to fight. Let God have it, and things are guaranteed to work out for your good. You are guaranteed to win. Why? Because all things work together for the good of them that love the Lord and are called according to His purpose (Romans 8:28). You are called. You are chosen for God's purpose—to live and enjoy this gift of life to the fullest.

So I choose to be humble day by day, minute by minute. I choose NOT to retaliate when I find out things done during and after our marriage that I was unaware of. I choose to gracefully bow out and leave the past in the past. I cast my cares upon Jesus Christ because He cares for me. He knows exactly what, when, and how to do.

I see it now. For so long I fought in my own strength. I fought to make him love me. I fought to make him see me when I became invisible to him. I fought. And my fight was enough because it kept me sane. My fight is what allowed me to walk away humbled but still with my dignity.

The call to humility is not the end. It is not for you to be humiliated. You will not be the laughing stock of your town, your church, your community, your circle of friends.

God promises that He will exalt you in due time. There is a set time where God will lift you up in a manner to bring glory to Him, and ALL THE WORLD WILL SEE!

"But the God of all grace, who hath called us unto his eternal glory by Christ Jesus, after that ye have suffered a while, makes you perfect, stablish, strengthen, settle you" (1 Peter 5:10).

I can rest now knowing it won't be like this always. You can rest upon the promise of a new day—a new beginning. God said it and that's enough for me. Good night or should I say, good morning. I smile as I lie back down knowing my promise is here! The hard times are over! And my new life has begun! I am blessed!

PERSEVERE! FIGHT!

"We're fighters, never gonna give up, never gonna give in! I'll take your hand and you'll take mine. We'll conquer this thing they call life! We're fighters! Yeah! Yeah! Yeah!"

Day 2—Yes, I'm still in day 2! I slept over half of the day away due to feeling under the weather from a cold bug I picked up from the preschoolers over Thanksgiving break. But as I stood at the side of my bed to get my day started, these words screamed loudly in my ear! "We're fighters! Yeah! Yeah! Yeah! Fighters!" And all throughout today, no matter how much Nyquil, Allegra, and Tylenol were in my system, nothing could dull this sense of perseverance and fight I felt in my spirit!

I am almost, almost totally free! I am moments away from the day I've waited so long for—the day I will officially be returned to me! How can one be so excited about the legal declaration of a divorce? I thought on how I frowned upon the times I heard of women throwing divorce parties. How could one celebrate such an occasion, such a loss? I even became angry once at a lady in a neighboring town, but my oh my, God has a way of humbling us to a greater understanding and a greater level of empathy and compassion for people and their situations. I, like the other women I once frowned upon (out of sheer ignorance of course), am not celebrating the act of divorce but the fact that I MADE IT! We celebrate the mere fact that we fought and survived the lonely nights, the acts of abuse and neglect, the feelings of shame and defeat as we fought what we felt was a losing battle! But oh, to lose just to win again! We didn't realize we were losing to gain, or else we would have fought with a completely different attitude!

We were losing that what had held us back, that what was robbing us of dear life. Yet through our fight, we gained ourselves back! We gained our motivation back! We gained our confidence back! We gained the gift of life back!

There's an old song that says no one knows the trouble I see; nobody knows my sorrows. This is so true for each individual. No one knows the truth of what goes on behind closed doors except you, your partner, and God! No one knows the extent of pain and disappointment you experience except you and God. Even the one causing the pain doesn't truly know the extent of their actions. But to make it through! To come out of a situation and be able to hold your head up, to make it out of dire distress, ALIVE…that in itself is enough to rejoice about! It doesn't matter HOW you came out but only that you're out! You persevered! You endured! And now you are ready for your new life!

You have fought the fight! You have kept the faith! You have finished your course! And NOW you are ready to be offered up into the new life that awaits you!

God did not bring you this far to leave you!

Know that your test is now a testimony because you endured. You persevered. You may have come out with wounds and bruises but know that God heals! Again, it doesn't matter HOW you came out! Just rejoice that you made it out alive!

When I looked the song up on Google (as I always do), I was shocked as I read the songwriter's testimony. She was laid in a hospital just two years prior as a victim of domestic violence. She said it was then that her eyes came open, and she decided to fight. She'd persevered and endured silently in a marriage to someone who didn't love her like Christ loved the church! Then she decided to fight and help others fight!

So I encourage you not to quit now that you're out! There is a champion in you! You always win! And God WILL use you to HELP someone else fight and win also!

I am victorious! You are victorious! WE are victorious!

ACCEPTANCE

November 2017—one day before the court hearing for the judge to finally sign and decree the legal dissolution of our marriage. I've shed some tears, but as I cried, I prayed and praised. My heart no longer hurts. My soul no longer aches. I have FULLY accepted that the marriage is over. As I wrote the date, I couldn't help but wonder what I was doing at this time during our first year of marriage. I actually almost wrote the year. LOL! My mind gently went back to what was then my reality. I kept seeing a picture of me in my red charmeuse with my hands covering my face. I wasn't crying, but I was recovering.

We'd rented a beach house on Tybee Island for our families to celebrate our first Thanksgiving together as one. Until this day, I don't remember what happened, but of course it was something I'd done that "caused" him to not to want me to touch him. I can remember us laughing and joking outside in front of everyone but him literally not wanting me to touch him nor talk to him in our bedroom. So nobody knew the trouble, the pain, the agony, the discord, nor the discontent that was really going on and what I was really feeling. But "SMILE" so no one will pick up on the fact that I was truly hurting in a way that I had no idea how to handle. So early one morning, I walked out to the beach with hopes of seeing the sunrise. It was cold, extremely cold, and honestly, too cold for anyone to be out on the beach, but I had to get away. I had to get by myself or at least where it was only me and God, so I could let it all out with a good cry! I needed to release the pain I was feeling. I can vividly see myself sitting on the beach with my knees curled up to my chest, feeling like I couldn't take anymore. I was ready to walk away because I was tired of the pain of rejection and displeasure within our marriage. I shuddered! I cried! My teeth chattered! And yet I cried some more! I had to get it out! I was distraught and didn't know what to do! Our marriage was nothing like I'd expected it to be! I'd never felt a pain so deep! But once I got my tears out, I was able to pick myself up and head back to the house.

To my surprise when I entered in, my mother and his mother were in the lowest section of the house praying. They both said the Holy Spirit woke them up and told them to go downstairs and pray. They both obeyed not realizing they would meet the other down there. They touched and agreed spiritually. They began to pull down strongholds. Neither of them knew I was out on the beach alone crying in desperation.

That meeting of the prayer warriors gave me the strength I needed to go on. I knew God had heard my prayer and my plea! And I knew I was NOT fighting alone! I had a renewed confidence that things would somehow get better, and they did! His attitude changed toward me. He went from not wanting me to touch him to being playful and peaceful, but it was only temporary.

We had so many moments like this where things would be going sour and God would come in and make a move. Divine intervention would always somehow step in. SO HOW IS IT THAT WE'RE GOING TO DIVORCE COURT TOMORROW? There is something very powerful called—CHOICES!

Life is full of choices! The Bible even tells us to choose ye this day whom we will serve! Our marriage came down to the powerful choice to follow SELF-will instead of GOD's will! And that my friend, is disobedience! I learned a long time ago that God's will is what's best for me, and I will never be dissatisfied with God's choices for me! No, I am not perfect! But even when I don't want what God wants for me, I try my best to submit and pray asking Him to do what needs to be done in me that I may accept and be happy with His will for me. It is my faith and confidence that God knows exactly what He's doing that has gotten me this far in life!

When I first awakened on this morning, I felt so free! I had so much peace until I literally did not know what to do. I gathered my divorce documents for tomorrow, reviewed them, and made certain all my ducks were in a row. I was ready to go!

I'm a fighter, and this I know quite well! My marriage was not a failure! It was ministry, and it served its purpose! No, I was not perfect in the marriage. I learned a lot! I grew a lot! But the marriage was ministry. God used me to extend His grace, love, and mercy unto my soon-to-be ex-husband. No matter how bad things got, God would always soften my heart toward him with forgiveness. Even during the darkest hours, God would always somehow come in and fix things. It wasn't always an immediate fixing of his attitude or actions. Many times it was a fixing of me, my attitude, my perception. God allowed me to go deeper. He showed me the deep things within that contributed to personalities and actions.

The marriage was ministry. It set me apart and showed me another side of God that I honestly had not seen before. It taught me to seek the why behind a lot of things. It also showed me that I am stronger than what I'd given myself credit for. I lived through the one thing I'd always said would tear me apart. I SURVIVED a bad marriage! I also learned the difficult lesson that sometimes people will be propelled by self-will. It's not that God didn't have great things in store for us! It's not that God didn't offer deliverance and change! I even believe there were points where God's offer of deliverance was accepted, but the choice was continuously made to continue returning to the old way of doing things, the old way of living.

I somehow feel like he felt like he was getting smarter and smarter. Great things were happening in his life, so he didn't need me anymore. I don't even think he turned his back on God. I do think he chose and wanted to do things his own way. I believe I HAD A CHOICE! I believe God said, "ENOUGH IS ENOUGH!" And God gave me a choice. I could either accept the way of escape He'd finally provided, or I could have stayed and prayed! I could have accepted that my deliverance was now, or I could have chosen to go around that mountain for a little while longer. I had to let go of fear. I had to let go of the pain and disappointment of the harsh reality that things didn't work out how I'd planned, and I accepted that God knew all the while what the end of this thing would be even before the beginning.

Our marrying each other was a choice. I remember I was so reluctant and afraid because something within me just knew that he was going to end up hurting me, but I was told, "so what if he does? That's just a risk you're gonna have to take." And I did. I trusted God with my all and married what I think sometimes was out of His will. LOL! I'm laughing, yes! I think this marriage was allowed because of another choice that affected God's original plan for me, but I've learned a lot!

GRACE comes clearly to me. God somehow graced me to live out my heart's desires. I desired to be married to my college sweetheart, and I did. I married the first guy I became involved with at Georgia Southern.

Now it is of utter importance that I seek God for his original plan and purpose to be fulfilled in my life. I'm tired of going around in circles. I'm tired of the permissive, what is allowed. I'm ready for the good and perfect will of the Father for my life, and I honestly believe I have that now. I'm on my way to BETTER!

DELIVERANCE

Remember not the former things,
  nor consider the things of old.
Behold, I am doing a new thing;
  now it springs forth, do you not perceive it?
I will make a way in the wilderness
  and rivers in the desert. (Isaiah 43:18–19)

Day 1

It's approximately 1:20 a.m. and I'm scrolling through my social media page. I came upstairs to prepare for bed, but somehow the cold medication energized me instead of making me sleepy. After watching a video about women dressing inappropriately, I decided to check out some of my pictures to determine if what was said pertained to me. As I scrolled, I made a bold decision to do something I don't think I'd done before. I decided to look at each album of myself and my soon-to-be ex-husband: pictures of pre-wedding planning, our wedding and reception, events we attended, fun family moments. They were all there, and I felt the smiles. I felt the joy. I felt the genuineness. I realized nothing I posted was fake nor pretend. Everything was real. It was all real! I loved my husband, and he once loved me too! So what happened? How did we get to this point while experiencing such joyous moments? We were once happy!

One word rang strongly in my spirit: "DISOBEDIENCE!" The demise of our marriage hinged upon nothing other than a choice to disobey the Lord. We made it through the adultery. We made it through the lonely nights when we didn't quite see eye to eye. We made it through the balancing of finances that we were told would surely take us out. We made it through all of the heavy hitters young couples are forewarned about. The extent of grace, mercy, and love shown during our marriage was nothing short of amazing. But there came a conscious decision that was made—a decision that said life will be better without the one who loves you unconditionally. A decision was made saying this was no longer the life he wanted to live. We were no longer worth it.

God knew my husband's heart when he told me to take a stand and speak up. The only request I was told to make was for him to meet my basic needs as his wife, and he immediately turned saying, "it's time for us to separate." Even after thoughtful consideration and attempting beyond my better judgement to give him one more chance, he declared again, "SEPARATION!"

Although those words were a dagger to my heart, they were also music to my ears. My deliverance was finally nigh! I no longer had to wonder about the status of our marriage. I now knew. It also eased the burden within me of knowing something was wrong during the marriage but constantly telling myself it was just me and my crazy thoughts.

So now that I'm here, I must be careful! I must be mindful to not be as many of the slaves were when their emancipation was declared. I must be careful to keep my eyes on the prize and focus on the deliverance that's nigh. The new thing has already begun and will soon be in complete fruition if I faint not. I cannot consider only the happy moments but must acknowledge the entire picture of our marriage. Sometimes emotions will cause us to choose and act unwisely. I see my Promised Land, and it is important that I not only see it, but I live in it. It's a must that I go all the way through, unto the very end of this thing that I may live and enjoy God's new way of life for me. I'm ready for life in His will done His way! I've learned I am never disappointed with His choice for me.

I dried my tears, held my head high, and recognized the difference in my cry once again. This time it was a cry of thanksgiving. This time it was a cry from my head, not my heart. My heart is still guarded within, and I will praise God all the way to my Promised Land.

WE'RE FIGHTERS

5:42 AM.

I can't say I dreamed about much on last night, but I can say I had a wonderful night. I am off to a great start to my day. My friend came over yesterday after work and things were a little tense. When I heard him pull into the driveway, I felt like I should have run downstairs and greeted him! But instead I went to the bathroom and began to prepare my bath. Crazy, right? Anyway, he moved the dresser and large chest from my bedroom into the other room to prepare for the delivery of the new bedroom set on Friday. You could feel the tension between us from the previous night as we'd disagreed about a personal decision he'd made. He finally decided to address the elephant in the room, and it went from there! Long story short, we ended up in a deep conversation. At the beginning he threatened to leave, and I told him I would not stop him! My reason for not stopping him is I had to take my hands out and let God put HIS hands in! I could NOT do ANYTHING of myself! But we talked. He was honest about some things, and so was I.

As I listened to him pour his heart out about his experiences and how he's seeing another side of people, I was reminded of my darkest hours when he'd been there for me. I was reminded of how he didn't allow me to cry alone, how he got down on the floor with me and let me snot and cry on his shoulder. So I did the same for him! I listened! And I positioned myself to be there for him! He began to reflect on how good God has been to him! I'm amazed sometimes at how I was with him for so long, umpteen years ago, but did not see certain parts of him, as if I took him for granted way back then! But I promise not to do that now! I love this man and cherish what we are building. Anyway, once we got through that incident, he said something so significant. He told me God showed him and told him I was his wife before he graduated from high school! That's when my mind went back to the proposal he did when I was in the tenth grade. I still remember the ring! We were engaged in HIGH SCHOOL. LOL! My laughter is joy!

On yesterday/last night after all the sharing and comforting and getting ourselves back together again, the Holy Spirit came in. We became positive again! He said he felt like running! I told him to do it—RUN! AND HE DID! He ran downstairs and ran around in the living room and dining room area! I cheered him on! I clapped my hands and began to praise God! I jumped for joy and began to thank God! I thanked Jesus! And we let the Lord have His way! As I looked on, all I could think about was how I'd always wondered and wanted the possibility of the Holy Spirit moving upon me and my husband within our home at the same time! I've always wanted to know if it was possible and how it would feel. This let me know it would feel GOOD! It felt right! And to see a man praise God freely the way I do when I'm alone at home—PRICELESS! I was amazed and overjoyed! My mind went back to when God told my uncle He sits upon the throne of my home! My mind went back to when God said, "this is a house of praise!" Oh, how wonderful it is! So what the enemy meant for bad turned out for good! And he began to speak, "Greater! The Lord said GREATER!" My soul cries out Hallelujah! I know we have some ways to go, but I thank God for us being here! I thank God that I finally truly have a man who He sits upon the throne of his heart. I don't have to wonder about his salvation. I know he's saved! I know he loves God! I know he has a relationship with God! I know he follows Christ! So we will follow him! He even prayed that on yesterday!

No more looking back! We are moving forward! We are pressing toward the mark for the prize of our high calling in Christ Jesus! We will have a family after God's own heart! He is mine, and I am His! By the way, today is the day of my court date that my name is legally restored back to Shondra Nicole Davis! I smile!

Today is my YAY!!!

10:20 AM.

"This is why I love you! Oooh, this is why I love you! Because you love me! You love me!"

I woke up to this song singing sweetly to me. I sent it to my new, and he confirmed this is how he feels about me. It's amazing that even though today is the official legal end of me and my ex's former marriage, God doesn't have me focusing on that. Instead, He has me focusing on my new beginning. He has me focusing on true love! I asked my new about what he said on last night about God showing him I was his wife in high school (I had to ask to be sure! LOL!), and he replied with the same thing I wrote about him proposing to me when I was in the tenth grade. It's like he and I were always meant to be and that what God ordains, He will maintain! And this man has somehow always remained in my heart. I've always prayed for him as God lead me to. **Now let me make this clear, there was no adulterous contact between us nor were we even in constant contact with each other over the years. When he told me he was marrying someone else years ago, I was instructed by my mother to ask God to change my love for him into a brotherly love—and God did! Now that I've made that clear, let me continue.**

At different times, God would show me his heart and his misery in life without me. I even realize now that I was so angry and hurt by him that I somehow felt he deserved what he was going through, but I still prayed for him. Two years ago I cried for him at my best friend's wedding because of the discontentment I saw and felt from him. That may even be where my complete and true forgiveness toward him came in. He was always that guy from the time we met that I honestly felt was my original soul mate. And today, I am full of his love. I am full of God's love! My walls have come tumbling down!

I focus NOT on what I lost but ONLY on what I've GAINED! I've gained my life back! I've gained my love back! I've gained ME back! God even called me "QUEEN!"

GROUND ZERO

"I'm here to speak hope to you. If I made it, you can make it too! You may feel like life is over. I won't let you go. Together we'll make it through! We're fighters!"

Here we are at ground zero—the moment we've all been waiting for. Today is the day I officially return to Shondra Nicole Davis. So many thoughts have gone through my mind. I've reviewed the divorce documents to ensure nothing has been missed. I've contacted the court secretary to make sure there isn't anything else I would need to bring. I even contacted my sister asking for her to accompany me, but she will be interviewing for a new job at the time of my court appearance.

So, it's me and You, God. You said You will never leave me nor forsake me. Your Word says You go before me. Even yesterday I read Romans 8:31. "What shall we then say to these things? If God be for us, who can be against us?"

I am more than a conqueror!

I will not be defeated! I will walk in with my head held high, and my heart humbly bowed before The Lord!

I will stand strong! I am confident that You, my God, will bring this thing to completion!

Ground zero is where it all begins! I smile as I type knowing that I am truly victorious!

I smile knowing just how far God has brought me from!

I smile knowing just how much He has brought me through!

I smile knowing that today is the first day of my new beginning!

Today is the day of my restoration!

Victory is here, and it feels great!

I have fought the good fight. I have kept the faith. I have finished the course that was set before me.

I have lost so that I may win!

I LOSE TO WIN!!!

CHOOSE HAPPY

As I walked out the courtroom, my eyes began to swell with tears. My name had been restored. I am officially Shondra Nicole Davis again! The divorce is final, but here come emotions! Before the tears could fall, it caught my eye. There sitting on a bench was a young lady with a bag with bold writing stating CHOOSE HAPPY! I received it immediately and began to walk forward and what happened? I dropped my keys right in front of her. Knowing what this meant, I turned to her and told her thank you. I told her I was about to cry until I saw her bag. CHOOSE HAPPY! I choose happy! She encouraged me simply with her words, "There you go!" Head high! Heels high! I am moving forward!

I wore heels today for the first time in ten months! Head high, heels high as I walked to my car! My new red Mercedes—a reminder that my life has gotten better and better! Exhale!

My life is getting better and better!

I am me again! I am healed! I am healthy!

I am prosperous! I don't look like what I've been through! No one knows what I've lost but can only see what I've gained!

Today is a new day! I will embrace and receive ALL that is in it for me!

SCRIPTURE

"For you shall go out in joy and be led forth in peace; the mountains and the hills before you shall break forth into singing, and all the trees of the field shall clap their hands" (Isaiah 55:12). "For God has not given us the spirit of fear and timidity, but of power, love, and sound mind" (2 Timothy 1:7).

MAKE PRAISE A PRIORITY

The Spirit of the Lord God is upon me
Because the Lord has anointed *and* commissioned me

To bring good news to the humble *and* afflicted;

He has sent me to bind up [the wounds of] the brokenhearted,

To proclaim release [from confinement and condemnation] to the [physical and spiritual] captives

And freedom to prisoners,

To proclaim the favorable year of the Lord,
And the day of vengeance *and* retribution of our God,

To comfort all who mourn,

To grant to those who mourn in Zion *the following*: To give them a turban instead of dust [on their heads, a sign of mourning], The oil of joy instead of mourning,

The garment [expressive] of praise instead of a disheartened spirit.

So they will be called the trees of righteousness [strong and magnificent, distinguished for integrity, justice, and right standing with God],

The planting of the Lord that He may be glorified." (Isaiah 61:1–3, Amplified Bible)

And that's what God has done for me and will do for you! You have just read my personal journal entries during the toughest, saddest, worst, yet GREATEST time of my life! How can I use all of these words that are so different and contradictory to each other to give a true account of my experience? Because that's exactly what was going on during this time in my life! This is EXACTLY what happens in each of our lives! As humans, we are not exempt from trials, tribulations, turmoil, etc., but as BELIEVERS, we are GUARANTEED that our losses are truly Christ's gain! We can only experience the gain if we faint not and endeavor to be on The Lord's side!

GOD has the final say! JEHOVAH, El Shaddai, God Almighty has the final say! HE knows the final outcome! So praise God because it gets better from here!

God is removing ALL of the ashes of what you've gone through or are going through and replacing it with a crown of BEAUTY!

YOU drip in the oil of joy! And JOY becomes STRENGTH! Walk in IT!

There is a PROMISE upon your life that is guaranteed to lead to PURPOSE if you are PERSISTENT!

DON'T throw in the towel yet! Actually, make up in your mind to NEVER THROW IN THE TOWEL!

Stay purpose minded and keep your mind on the promise!

A focal point provides an incentive to continue, to keep going, to move forward!

Sometimes step by step, inch by inch, moment by moment, day by day, you do whatever it takes to help you move forward from your loss to your gain! The important thing is to NEVER STOP! NEVER QUIT!

Put a praise on your lips! If you can't stop crying, put a praise in your hands (wave, clap, point, whatever it takes!) Also remember that God understands your tears! But whatever you do, purposely somehow tell God thank you even if it's only in your thoughts.

You're gonna make it! Not only will you make it but YOU WILL WIN! YOU WILL GAIN THE BETTER THAT GOD HAS FOR YOU!

SCRIPTURE

Beloved, do not be surprised at the fiery ordeal which is taking place to test you [that is, to test the quality of your faith] as though something strange *or* unusual were happening to you. But insofar as you are sharing Christ's sufferings, keep on rejoicing so that when His glory [filled with His radiance and splendor] is revealed, you may rejoice with great joy. (1 Peter 4:12–13)

NO STRESS ZONE

Don't worry about anything; instead, pray about everything; tell God your needs, and don't forget to thank him for his answers. If you do this, you will experience God's peace, which is far more wonderful than the human mind can understand. His peace will keep your thoughts and your hearts quiet and at rest as you trust in Christ Jesus. (Philippians 4:6–7)

The past few days have been quite interesting. So many things have come to me that would and should cause me to fear. It's like the devil wants to steal my joy. The weekly worker's compensation checks I have been used to are no longer coming. Things have been on edge in my new relationship. Christmas is right around the corner, and I should be wondering if and how I will purchase gifts for my loved ones, my daughter mainly. I was even told two days ago of a plot formed years ago to harm me.

But even in all of this, I have a choice to make. I can choose to focus on things I don't have with anxiety, or I can choose to be confident in what I already know God is able to do. I choose the latter!

There are so many people hurting all around us. I've received so many phone calls and messages of those who are at their wit's end with situations in life. I find myself telling them over and over about the power of choices. We as human beings have the power to CHOOSE how we react to a situation. We can choose to play worst-case scenarios repeatedly in our minds or accept the blessed assurance God has given us.

In the verse above, Paul gives the people a few simple instructions:

1. Be anxious for NOTHING! Don't stress about ANYTHING, NOTHING!
2. Pray! Talk to God about your needs. Tell God all about it!
3. Don't forget to tell The Lord thank you!

We have to approach life knowing that God is able to do whatever it is we stand in need of. This is not a cliché! This is LIFE! When we trust God, our attitudes change. Our stress level changes. That what seems impossible becomes possible. That what seems a dream becomes reality.

He goes on to say IF you do this, follow these three simple steps when facing things in life; there is a peace from God that will come upon you. Your mind will stop wandering. Your heart will not fear! You will no longer be afraid! It is not healthy for one to stress!

How do you do it? I'm glad you asked!

For every negative thought, think on something positive. What is something positive that has happened to you today or yesterday if you're just starting your day off? Have your answer yet? Come on. Think harder. It may be something simple that you need to make great. Got it? Now smile and think about it!

What is a prayer God answered for you in the past? What is something that seemed impossible that it would be done but it happened? Got it? Think about that!

What is something that stressed you to the max before but had a positive outcome? Got it? Think on That!

Think on these things immediately when worries and fears try to take over.

Changing our mind-set is half the battle.

You can make it! You WILL make it! All is well and will continue to be well in the No Stress Zone!

IT'S TIME TO GROW

Today my sister, the licensed cosmetologist, planned on visiting me. I was super excited to share with her my new-found joy. I'd removed the weave from my hair the day before and surprised by the fact that my hair had grown greatly since the beginning of the year. My hair was the longest it had ever been in my life! So I pulled my hair down out of the ponytail holder and began to show off for her (this is what me and my sister do constantly, show off for each other when we have something new).

Anyway, I was surprised at her response but honestly expected it. LOL! She began to congratulate me on the hair growth but also informed me that I would need to cut my split/dead ends for my hair to continue to grow properly. I of course resisted because I was so excited! But her next words to me stuck like glue and set a wildfire in my heart! She simply said, "What you need to understand is that your hair is growing and is capable of growth, but you have to cut it so it can grow correctly and healthy."

Wow!

And such is life! Sometimes certain things have to be cut away from us in order for us to continue to GROW! Growth is an essential part of life. Without growth and renewal, one would become stagnant and die out.

Pruning, a synonym for cutting, means to cut away dead or overgrown branches or stems (things attached to your life) to increase fruitfulness and growth; reduce the extent of something by REMOVING superfluous or unwanted parts. (Webster's Dictionary Online)

Will you be cut on today? Will you allow God to prune you into your promises? Will you allow God to remove whatever dead is in your life so that you may grow healthily and correctly into the next level of your life? Will you CHOOSE to grow?

SCRIPTURE

> Don't give holy things to depraved men. Don't give pearls to swine! They will trample the pearls and turn and attack you. (Matthew 7:6)

SCRIPTURE

> Every branch in Me that does not bear fruit, He takes away and every branch that bears fruit He prunes that it may bear more fruit. (John 15:2).

It's TIME TO GROW!

IMAGE

Today is a great day! Today is an awesome day!

Today is the day our God has made, and I will rejoice and BE GLAD in it!

Heading to the doctor on this morning, I quickly brushed my hair back, put a hat on, threw on a pair of tights, tennis shoes, and a matching shirt. I of course made sure I was cute(LOL) but also felt very relaxed. While driving, the thought came to me on how I used to dress verses how I dress now. Why is that? Why am I so comfortable in tennis shoes and a hat? Why didn't I feel the need to put on a dress, some slacks, or some type of business attire for my doctor's appointment?

And that's when the word came to me: IMAGE! I no longer have to hold to a certain IMAGE. I can be me!

Previously I served as the Director of Operations of a major health care agency in Savannah and always knew to be on guard at all times. I stayed prepared to represent the company well just in case I encountered a potential client or patient. I carried myself to ensure the company would be proud to acknowledge me as their local leader.

I also served as a wife to a man who stressed the importance of image to him. "Image is everything," he would say. So of course, I wanted to make and keep my husband proud, and I definitely wanted to represent him well. I wanted the world to know that I, Shondra Nicole Stewart, was holding the standard of perfection and dignity set by my man! No time to relax because I never knew who would see me!

Don't get me wrong, I was and am everything I portrayed. I hold fast to the belief that if one will just BE, then the correct image will be portrayed in their daily life. Yet, I didn't allow myself to relax. Notice I said *I* didn't allow myself to relax. It's not so much that I was instructed that this was required, yet now that I think about it, there were certain "images" and "expectations" set by people other than myself. Regardless of if these things were openly expressed or indirectly implied, standards were set and I wanted to meet them—I needed to meet them.

But today, I fully understand I've always met those standards and some I even exceeded! It's never been about how beautiful my clothes were or how perfect my hair was. It is my inner beauty that illuminates whatever walk of life I'm in!

So today, I lose my image! I relinquish that thing that tells me I must provide the picture-perfect image to prove I am worthy of my positions in life. I will no longer feel the need to dress the part, look the part, nor act the part! I will focus on BEING the part because I AM the part!

Today, I lost my image and you should too!

SCRIPTURE

> "And I will cut off your carved images and your pillars from among you, and you shall bow down no more to the work of your hands" (Micah 5:13).

PERFECT PEACE

It seems all hell has tried to break loose in my life. This morning, I was awakened by a dream that stimulated a very interesting conversation between myself and my newly-restored love. I kept feeling that he was holding something back but never could quite put my finger on it. After sharing my dream with him on this morning, some very interesting things came out. He is dealing with fear—the fear of letting go and fully moving on. It seemed there is so much riding on this relationship. I just knew that it would be through this man that we would finally live the life God promised. I just knew that he was my promise returned after so many years of being stolen away. And now THIS?!? Now he reveals that he's been secretly battling with how to move forward. The love is there. The commitment is there, yet his commitment and loyalty are on a greater level for something else.

I began to ask God why. I felt pretty numb at first. But considering the most recent events of my life, I definitely don't want to try to make something happen that's not meant to be. And I DON'T want to place something TEMPORARY into a PERMANENT position!

God, You've shown me so much about this man. You've shown me his love for me. You told me to open my heart to him, open my life to him. And now, we are here. Where do I go? What do I do?

It's about 3 p.m. and I promise you the sun looks dull outside. I honestly thought I had my man back! LOL! Where did all of this come from?

So now I have a choice. Do I respond in fear? Or do I respond in faith?

Fear says, "Sit around, mope, and wait for his decision."

Faith says, "GET UP AND GO MAKE THIS A GREAT DAY!"

Its nine days before Christmas, and there is some joy out there I need to tap into! There is some life out there I need to experience! Will I waddle in pity thinking of the fact that this relationship too may be coming to an end? Or will I get up, put some pep in my step, and continue to walk into the blessings God has for me?

My tire went flat on last night for no reason while my daughter was heading to the game. I'm sitting at the place now to have it replaced. That's $60 out of my budget—I really didn't plan for. I haven't bought the first Christmas gift because money is so tight, and I no longer get the workers' compensation checks.

But in spite of it all, God, I STILL give YOU the praise! I still give YOU the glory!

I honor YOU with every step I take!

I choose FAITH over fear! Even as I type, I feel myself smiling! This is one of the "all times" that I will bless The Lord!

SCRIPTURE

"Thy will keep thee in perfect peace whose mind is stayed on thee" (Isaiah 26:3).

WHAT HE SAID

As I awakened on this morning, the word Zebulon rang constantly in my spirit. Knowing it's a place in the Bible, I proceeded to google it of course! I was expecting something long and drawn out, but it was really short, sweet, and right to the point.

Zebulon means home, to settle a matter, dwelling place, exalted, honored—And that's honestly what I feel! Zebulon was also one of the twelve tribes of Israel. Also as I read, I learned Zebulon was exalted by God but at sometimes, failed to obey God completely. But each time they would come to their senses and return to obedience. God even honored Zebulon by allowing Christ's first teachings to take place in their land (Galilee).

I want to honor God in all that I do, say, and am. I realized on last night the connection between me looking for love and beginning to experience heartaches and heartbreaks on a totally different level once my first love married someone else all of those years ago. Prior to that, I knew that somehow he and I would end up back together no matter how long or how far we were apart. We were God's original plan for each other's life, but his marriage to someone else was so final! I remember clearly saying it opened me up to a whole new world. I began to search for love—the love that was taken from me. And my, my, my did I go through it! I experienced heartbreak after heartbreak. I thought heartbreaks were over when I totally surrendered to Jesus, but it somehow crept back in basically because I constantly searched and wondered about my husband, who he would be, and how it would happen.

Anyway, I finally got what I desired! Yet it didn't work out how I wanted it to, despite me giving it my all! I am amazed as I write this because not one tear has come nor one pain in my heart.

This weekend has been nothing short of amazing! The Holy Spirit had me to engage in love. On Friday morning, I constantly heard the song "Why I Love You" by Major. Finally that morning while leaving out of Wal-Mart, I began to ask what I should do. How do I handle this what I'm hearing? How do I handle this what is trying to take place? And I gently heard the Holy Spirit whisper, "Embrace it! Engage in it!" And at that moment, I committed to doing just that! I told the Lord I will and also asked that He shows me how. I opened myself up to love, to receive the love I'd been waiting and searching so long for.

It seemed like all hell broke loose around me immediately with other situations erupting to steal my joy and try to detour my focus. My family, my friend, everyone was at each other's throats! But I was DETERMINED to not miss my moment! Like Joel Osteen says, "This was a defining moment!" I came home, turned my love music playlist on of songs the Holy Spirit had given me/us over time. (It's a good idea to keep a playlist of songs that inspire you so you can go back to them as needed.) I began to clean and organize my clothes. Although I wasn't supposed to, I moved the mattress and night stand out of my room and vacuumed the floor. The delivery guys were scheduled at any time to bring the new bedroom set, and I began to get EXCITED! I rejoiced and cried tears of thanksgiving! Mr. New and I joked through text messages. We both kept telling each other just how much we loved each other and are happy to be back together again! I was CHOOSING TO BE HAPPY!

I chose not to focus on what I'd lost but only on the new love and the new life I'd gained! I take that back—I focused on the renewed love! I focused on all things being made NEW! Our bed was delivered and set up! I say our bed even though he isn't a resident here with me yet, but I see what God is doing! I was so excited when he got home! Yes, home! My home will soon be his home! This for now will be our home! It took us going to about four or five different stores, but we finally found a comforter set we both loved and agreed on. WE fixed our bed TOGETHER! And waking up the next morning was like a dream come true. It felt like a fairy tale or something I'd seen on a music video, but it was real! And it's lasting!

I cooked breakfast for us, more like brunch because it was about 12 p.m. when we ate. The feeling I had when I opened my eyes on yesterday morning was simply bliss! Actually he woke me up! And as I looked around, I could feel the difference. I could feel the new. I could feel that I was in a place I'd never been before! I was in TRUE LOVE!

It was like yesterday was an extension of our past, like we were living moments all over again. I even felt something while hugging him that I hadn't felt since my teenage years, TRUE SECURITY! Oh yeah, and when he kissed me while we were in Marshall's Friday night, it was as if electricity (honestly the anointing) went all through my body! I felt like shouting!

As we talked yesterday morning, sweet memories and moments began to come back to me. I began to remember the good things, and I truly believe I will begin to remember more! I don't have to fight painful memories of our past that were honestly precious moments I allowed to become pain of disappointment. I can think about the good times now because it's so clear that we are building upon them. He's forty years old, and I'm thirty-eight. We've missed a lot, yet I know we gained a lot. The experiences of our past, both good and bad have prepared us for our future. We are back in stride again. My eyes focused on the words at the bottom of the page in my journal: "Optimism is a happiness magnet. If you stay positive, good things and good people will be drawn to you."

It's God's will for me to be happy! It's God's will for YOU to be happy!

He watched football literally ALL day yesterday! But he still had a way of seeing me as he watched the games; I never felt left out. I never felt alone. I even made him some dip, bought us some wings, and bought his favorite drink. Amazingly both of our favorite wings are lemon pepper. He absolutely loved the dip, and the tiny cans of Cherry Coke were perfect! He never left the house but found his spot on the couch and contently stayed there! Yes, he got up for bathroom breaks! LOL! I knew exactly what to do! I put on a shirt of his favorite team (University of Georgia), sat with him at times, and tried not to talk too much. I finally fell asleep across his lap around 9:30 or so and didn't wake up until after 11. Basically, it was a day well spent!

I got a call from my sister, and we somehow began talking about relationships. We talked about my recent divorce and what led to it. She shared a lot of personal things with me that she'd only shared with God and a select few. I could only tell her what and how I was led to tell her by God's Holy Spirit and wisdom. In the end, she said that was the first time she'd gotten clarity about her situation. She used the words that it was like Jesus Himself came into her van, sat with her, and listened to her. She left with an understanding from God and a peace. I prayed for her as she talked and expressed herself to me. I realize and know that I am nothing without God in me!

Twice yesterday, I was told in so many words to open up and let God take me higher, so I can touch lives in the capacity He wants me to! And I in turn said, "I yield!" As I was crying/praying before God on this morning, I heard "Pastor anointing. Double portion." Again, I kindly oblige and will continue to seek His will and His way! I love being used by God! Even on Friday, a former employee asked me am I about to go into ministry full time. He also encouraged me as he told the difference Jesus within me made in his life and in the agency I was the director over. It is a true blessing when you have truly been used by God and when Jesus is evident in your life!

SCRIPTURE

> "For I know the plans *and* thoughts that I have for you," says the LORD, "plans for peace *and* well-being and not for disaster, to give you a future and a hope. Then you will call on Me, and you will come and pray to Me, and I will hear [your voice] *and* I will listen to you. Then [with a deep longing] you will seek Me *and* require Me [as a vital necessity] and [you will] find Me when you search for Me with all your heart. I will be

found by you," says the LORD, "and I will restore your fortunes and I will [free you and] gather you from all the nations and from all the places where I have driven you," says the LORD, "and I will bring you back to the place from where I sent you into exile" (Jeremiah 29:11–14, Amplified Bible).

GRACE AND MERCY

"Your grace and mercy brought me through. I'm living this moment because of You. I want to thank You and praise You too. Your grace and mercy brought me through!"

These are the words I found myself singing as I prepared for the day. I was performing my morning nuptials and suddenly realized I'd began singing out loud! Grace and mercy—two wonderful things I know I cannot live without!

Grace—the unmerited favor of God! It's nothing that I've earned but simply a gift God gives us to show Himself strong in our lives.

Mercy, woo! It's so breathtaking to know our God loves us so much that He overlooks our faults and sins and still blesses us as He sees fit!

And the great thing about them both is they're endless!

God loves us more than we can imagine! Through the night, I had dreams of mishaps and almost mishaps. For instance, I dreamed a male stylist was about to dry my hair using a towel that had tiny glass shavings on it. He couldn't see them but I could. He fought me tooth and nail trying to persuade me there was no glass, but I knew what I saw. I also knew that him using that towel on my head would be harm to me, so I had to speak up. That's how the mercy and grace of God works. He allows us to see harm and danger even when others don't see. He forewarns us of things to prevent harm from being done to us. He softens the blows of our enemies to keep us from destruction. HE CARES FOR US, and HE SHOWS IT!

Take a moment to reflect on all of the things that have happened to you. Have you ever experienced something you know should have taken you out or should have caused you to become depressed, disappointed, or defeated? But for some reason you came out on top. You became sad, but you didn't get depressed. Things didn't turn out the way you wanted but it still had a positive outcome. You were left unharmed! All of this is because of God's grace and mercy covering you throughout your life. We are who we are because of God's grace and mercy in our lives. We should live, move, and have our being in Him. Grace and mercy—the reasons we have our being! The way we WIN and GAIN!

SCRIPTURE

> "Surely, goodness [grace] and mercy shall follow me all the days of my life. And I will dwell in the house of the Lord forever" (Psalm 23:6).

REST

11:45 p.m.

Today I rested. I slept the majority of the day. A sleep fell upon me that I could not nor did I want to shake off. We watched church services via UStream. The highlight of today's sermon was God saying He is giving us beauty for ashes. He's giving us the oil of joy in the place of our spirit of heaviness.

I cried. We cried. And we praised! We praised God together! We spun around together!

Today I rested in the arms of my beloved like never before! It's like God Himself gave me peace from the battles! No more fighting! No more arguing! No more discouragement!

Only JOY, PEACE, LOVE, AND HAPPINESS!

Today I found rest for my weary soul!

I have labored!

I was heavy laden!

But I gave my problems to Jesus!

And He has given me REST!

SCRIPTURE

Come to Me, all who are weary and heavily burdened [by religious rituals that provide no peace], and I will give you rest [refreshing your souls with salvation]. Take My yoke upon you and learn from Me[following Me as My disciple], for I am gentle and humble in heart, and YOU WILL FIND REST [renewal, blessed quiet] FOR YOUR SOULS. For My yoke is easy [to bear] and My burden is light. (Matthew 11:28–30)

I WIN!!!!!!

"Have you ever needed someone so bad? But he wasn't willing to make it last. Sometimes you've got to lose to win again!"

It's 4:57 a.m. and those are the words singing in my head as I proceeded downstairs to make a cup of coffee. Yep, I was awakened and reminded of Mr. New's subtle hint last night that he'd love for me to make him some coffee on this morning before work. Why am I hearing these words? Anyway, a cup of coffee at four in the morning is nothing for the man who stayed in with me all weekend! I have no problem performing this simple gesture of love to seal our great weekend together!

He hadn't planned on staying until today, Monday morning but decided to when he realized I wasn't ready for him to leave. So little to my knowledge he'd made a trip to Goody's on yesterday and purchased a nice Polo shirt, a pair of khaki slacks, and appropriate shoes! ALL FOR ME!

So I made his cup of love. We prayed, gave a simple kiss, and out into the world he went! I pray he has a blessed day! As I proceed upstairs, I can only tell God, "THANK YOU FOR MY WIN! I WIN AGAIN!"

I will not focus on anything I've lost ONLY on what I'm WINNING! I WIN! I have a man who loves ME!

My mind returned to the message from my pastor on yesterday that said *Praise is in order now!* Focus on praising God because the thing that brought us ashes in 2017 is no longer! And GOD is giving us the oil of joy for our spirit of heaviness (Isaiah 61). He has given me beauty for ashes! I had to lose to win again! Yes, it was like something strange took place in my life! I lost my job! I lost my husband!

I lost my status in life! But I count it all joy because I STILL WIN! Literally, I STILL WIN!

I am receiving the desires of my heart! I own a new Mercedes CLK 350 special edition in my favorite color, TRUE RED! I have a brand-new luxurious king-sized canopy bed—something I've wanted since I was a little girl! My daughter is a freshman in college and currently on the Dean's List! And I am rekindling the relationship with the man of my dreams, my first love, my true heart's desire! EVERYTHING the enemy meant for my bad, GOD is truly turning it around and working it for my good! I'M WINNING!

I realized on this weekend that even my thought patterns are different. I remember things from my immediate past, but they seem so far removed from me. I realize I have a choice. I can either spend time and energy trying to force things back up, or I can accept the peace and move forward. I choose peace and newness! I hear, "Double for your trouble!" God is truly giving me double for my trouble! That's one of my favorite scenes in the movie, *Love and Basketball.* They're playing a game of one on one for his heart. She obviously loses, and the character "Q" says, "Double or nothing!" And the rest is history!

I am in the stage of double! I feel the anointing of double so strong that it wouldn't surprise me one bit if I end up having twins, a boy and a girl, when I get married again! LOL! At first I wasn't open to it, but the more I think on it, I begin to say, "Any way you bless me Lord, I'll be satisfied!" Even as I read Isaiah 61 in its entirety, I saw the anointing of double for your troubles! So I believe it and receive it in Jesus Name!

Another thing I realize is what I've experienced was not only for me but also for others. It's for the work of God's ministry through me. On the day the divorce decree was signed into law, confusion began to ensue. I received a call from a friend in distress about a situation that we've talked and prayed about repeatedly. I immediately gave to her what had just been given to me, the power to make the CHOICE to be happy! Later that night, confusion began to stir in the homes of my local family members. I received calls from couples arguing and fighting. Both the husband and wife had valid points, but how was I supposed to give them Godly advice when I'd just left divorce court myself? A mother and daughter arguing lead to the daughter now residing in my home. This doesn't seem fair right? Am I gonna be given a chance to embrace, enjoy, and regroup from my major life event? Hello! Does anyone care? But the phone calls and text messages kept coming from far and near. And LIFE kept happening!

It wasn't until Saturday night while I was talking to my baby sister that I got it! As I listened to the genuineness and sincerity about her search for guidance, for an answer, for relief, it hit me! THIS IS NOT ABOUT ME AT ALL! I was looking at this as a time of peace, a time of joy, a time for me to bask in the newness of life! And He gave me that! He let me feel the joy and the peace my new life was bringing. He let me feel the power behind the divorce being finalized legally! He allowed me to rejoice in my new gained freedom and deliverance! But what better way to show my appreciation and gratitude than to reach back and help pull someone else out of the fire?

It is our duty as human beings to do unto others as we would have done unto us! I could not close my doors and close myself off from the world! I wanted so badly to put my phone on do not disturb and just not answer calls, but I couldn't. There were hurting souls out there who needed me urgently, whose issues could not wait!

So I have GAINED once again! I realized God had empowered me with the tools to bring peace, life, and hope to others in dire situations. It was as my baby sister talked so openly and freely to me that I listened to the voice telling me it was not about me! LOL! Funny right? Even before she and I hung up the phone, my sister began to admonish me to accept the higher calling of Christ upon my life. She said to me, "You and God have something special. I don't know what you're waiting on. But Sis, open up so He can use you to touch the lives at the capacity He wants you to." Her words meant so much and held so much weight! Those words caused me to go before God with arms outstretched simply saying, "Lord, here I am! Use me for Your Glory! I yield and accept the higher calling You've placed upon my life!"

So I WIN AGAIN!

I've gained yet another high calling upon my life! I've gained yet another set of tools to add life to someone else's life!

I—WIN—AGAIN!

ABOUT THE AUTHOR

Shondra N. Davis is a native of Dublin–Georgia. She is the mother of two beautiful daughters, Love and Hope.

Shondra is a Registered Nurse and entrepreneur by trade but a Woman of God by choosing. She accepted the call as an ordained minister in 2008 and has served as a spiritual mentor and life advisor to many. Shondra is most passionate about motivating, encouraging, and helping others, especially women and young adults, to find and live their best life spiritually, physically, mentally, and naturally. Shondra's philosophy of life is this: God has outlined and ordained a specific life and purpose for each individual and will orchestrate events to ensure we find it. It will be there, in God's purpose that one will find the joy, peace, happiness, and abundance so many spend their entire lives searching for. All it takes is a simple yielding to and acceptance of God's will.

Shondra is no stranger to suffering and struggles as she was raised in a single-parent home by her Christian Mother, Lueretta. Shondra is the youngest of five children and herself became a single parent as a teenager, and has also been divorced. In spite of all of these and other life occurrences, Shondra knows and shows that with faith in God and perseverance, you CAN and WILL overcome all obstacles! And your overcoming will be that of VICTORY! One can live life in a manner that others will only know your story when you choose to tell, not because you look like what you've been through!

Our prayer is that this manuscript and the many others to come will serve as a blessing, as evidence, and most of all, MOTIVATION for you to press forward through all loss and difficult situations knowing that in the end YOU WILL WIN!

Printed in the USA
CPSIA information can be obtained
at www.ICGtesting.com
CBHW020831040824
12617CB00035B/448